Riddle-day Saints

Riddle-day Saints

Written by
Rick Walton

Illustrated by
Howard Fullmer

DESERET BOOK COMPANY
Salt Lake City, Utah

Library of Congress Cataloging-in-Publication Data

Walton, Rick.
Riddle-day saints / Rick Walton.
p. cm.
ISBN 0–87579–821–7
1. Riddles, Juvenile. 2. Mormon Church—Juvenile humor. 3. The Church of Jesus Christ of Latter-day Saints—Juvenile humor. [1. Riddles. 2. Jokes. 3. Mormon Church—Wit and humor. 4. The Church of Jesus Christ of Latter-day Saints—Wit and humor.] I. Title.
PN6371.5.W364 1994
818'.5402—dc20 93–47423
CIP
AC

Printed in the United States of America
10 9 8 7 6 5 4 3 2

To Rob and Dynette Reynolds
and their riddle ones,
Adam, Gwen, and Ben

Q: Where did the Jaredites get eggs?

A: From the Ether bunny.

Q: Which Church President tasted good?

A: Brigham Yum.

Q: How did happy dogs cross the plains?

A: *In waggin' trains.*

Q: What's green, preaches the gospel, and looks good on dinner plates?

A: *Parsley P. Pratt.*

Q: How did Brigham Young hear about what was going on in Salt Lake City?

A: *Through his pion-ears.*

Q: Why did Lehi and his family leave Jerusalem?

A: *Because it was too big to take with them.*

Q: Who puts the leaves back on the trees in the spring?

A: The Re-leaf Society.

Q: Which Church President was all right?

A: David M. Okay.

Q: What do shoemakers sing at their annual clearance sales?

A: "Know This, That Every Sole Is Free."

Q: What do you find at the end of life?

A: The letter e.

Q: When will confused people be resurrected?

A: *During the last daze.*

Q: Which President of the Church had a tough time in the summer?

A: *Lorenzo Snow.*

Q: What hymn do mountain climbers like to sing?

A: "High on the Mountain Top."

Q: Why do Mormons treat coffee like dirt?

A: Because it's ground.

Q: Where do stewardships sail?

A: On Free Agent Seas.

Q: Why were there only twenty-four letters in the alphabet when Joseph Smith was a boy?

A: Because we didn't have the D&C yet.

Q: Why did Adam fall?

A: *Because of the gravity of what he had done.*

Q: What kind of reptile do missionaries like to see?

A: *Investi-gators.*

Q: How did Mormon gymnasts cross the plains?

A: By handcartwheels.

Q: Why are righteous kings so good at measuring?

A: Because they're excellent rulers.

Q: What did all the pioneers grow when they came to the Salt Lake Valley?

A: Older.

Q: What's the Boy Scouts' favorite animal?

A: A merit badger.

Q: What's the favorite song of pirates?

A: "There is booty all around . . . "

Q: What is the dry cleaner's hymn?

A: "Let Us All Press On."

Q: What do you sing if you borrow lots of money from your dad?

A: "Owe My Father."

Q: What would Cleopatra be if she joined the Church?

A: A reformed Egyptian.

Q: What do you get if you cross Rice-a-Roni with an oyster?

A: A Pearl of Great Rice.

Q: Who keeps people quiet in church?

A: The hushers.

Q: What do you get if you cross a Bible, a bee, and a tree?

A: *Religious bee leafs.*

Q: Why do we believe in Enoch?

A: *Because he was translated correctly.*

Q: Who saw Joseph pray in the Sacred Grove?

A: The tree witnesses.

Q: Why wouldn't Brigham Young's kids quit drinking soft drinks?

A: Because they liked their pop.

Q: Why is Harold B. Lee like Nephi?

A: Because he was born of good Lee parents.

Q: How did Ammon take the king's enemies by surprise?

A: He disarmed them.

Q: What could Ammon have done that would have been even more effective than disarming the king's enemies?

A: *He could have de-feeted them.*

Q: Why was the ocean mad at Lehi?

A: Because Lehi crossed it.

Q: Who takes care of sick souls?

A: Doctor N. Covenants.

Q: Why were Laman and Lemuel never attractive?

A: *Because they were always revolting.*

Q: Where do Mormon ghosts live?

A: *In Nau-boo.*

Q: Why do Boy Scouts make good gymnasts?

A: Because they do good turns.

Q: Where are car thieves mentioned in the Bible?

A: When the Israelites took the fords of Jordan. (Judges 3:28.)

Q: Where do you find Mormon cattle?

A: *In the Beef Stake.*

Q: Who leads the Beef Stake?

A: *The steak president.*

Q: Who helps the steak president?

A: His cow-ncilors.

Q: Where do Mormon cows go to school?

A: BYMoo.

Q: Why do they go to BYMoo?

A: To play footbull.

Q: Why do the Rocky Mountains never worry?

A: Because they take everything for granite.

Q: What do Mormons think of crickets?

A: They think they're for the birds.

Q: Why does the letter *o* need to repent?

A: Because it's always in trouble *and never in* church.

Q: Why does Moroni stand on the Salt Lake Temple?

A: *Because he can't sit.*

Q: Why do thirteen-year-old Mormon girls have such good manners?

A: *Because they Beehive themselves.*

Q: Which artist found a husband because of her artwork?

A: Rebekah, whom Isaac married because she drew a pitcher of water. (Genesis 24.)

Q: Where are the best pasta recipes in the scriptures?

A: In the book of Macaroni.

Q: Who was the most dangerous pass defender in the Bible?

A: Edom, who told Moses, "Thou shalt not pass by me, lest I come out against thee with the sword." (Numbers 20:18.)

Q: What do ranchers sing on December 25?

A: "I Herd the Bulls on Christmas Day."

Q: Who makes sure Mormons pay their tithing?

A: The Eternal Revenue Service.

Q: Who is the dullest person in the Bible?

A: Jehoiada, who bored a hole. (2 Kings 12:9.)

Q: Why do we always refer to little lambs as being poor?

A: Because they're always gamboling.

Q: Why will the righteous be resurrected?

A: Because you can't keep a good man down.

Q: Why do we have keys to the kingdom instead of dials?

A: Because we're not supposed to have any secret combinations.

Q: What is the seagulls' favorite Southern recipe?

A: *Kentucky Fried Crickets.*

Q: Where do Mormon space creatures go to college?

A: *BYUFO.*

Q: Which is the richest river in the Bible?

A: The River Jordan, which overflowed all its banks. (Joshua 3:15.)

Q: What advice does the Bible give Santa Claus?

A: "Ho, ho, come forth, and flee from the land of the north." (Zechariah 2:6.)

Q: What did Mormon hairdressers sing as they crossed the plains?

A: "Comb, Comb, Ye Saints."

Q: What is the favorite song of Mormon librarians?

A: "Come, Let Us Renew."

Q: How can we tell that many of BYU's football players are returned missionaries?

A: They keep trying to convert third downs.

Q: How did Moses part the Red Sea?

A: With a sea-saw.

Q: Which Church President suited the Mormons best?

A: *John Tailor.*

Q: Why do pine trees have to repent?

A: *Because they are knotty.*

Brigham: Did you hear they found a giant oyster in Price, Utah?

Heber: No!

Brigham: And when they opened it up, do you know what they found?

Heber: No, what?

Brigham: The Great Pearl of Price.

Q: What do you call three hundred Mormons who travel and sing with Don Quixote?

A: The Mormon Tabernacle Squires.

Q: How do missionaries talk to Norwegians?

A: In Norse Code.

Q: What does every pirate have in the spirit world?

A: A spirit booty.

Q: Where do you go to learn to procrastinate?

A: Someday School.

Q: Where do aunts and uncles get together to cry?

A: At family re-onions.

Q: Which biblical pitcher was told to walk the batter?

A: *Noah, who was told to "pitch it within and without." (Genesis 6:14.)*

Q: Why do people look up to Moroni?

A: *Because he's on the ball.*

Q: What did the pioneers use to buy food?

A: Winter Quarters.

Q: What do visitors to Utah say when they see the mountains?

A: "O Ye Mountains, Hi!"

Q: What song do people sing who slump?

A: "The Lord My Posture Will Repair."

Q: How do you save your ancestors?

A: Through Genealogical Research and Rescue.

Q: How do raisins keep track of their genealogy?

A: *On family grape sheets.*

Q: Who presides over a family tree?

A: *The branch president.*

Q: What should you do if you don't like to sing in church?

A: Use a humbook.

Q: What common family name today was not found among the Israelites?

A: "There was no smith found throughout all the land of Israel." (1 Samuel 13:19.)

Q: Where did Laman and Lemuel go to dance?

A: To a Lamanightclub.

Q: What kind of dishes did J. Golden Kimball use for dining?

A: J. Golden Plates.

Q: Which song tells about a big heavenly insect?

A: "I Saw a Mighty Angel Fly."

Q: Where does the Bible say you shouldn't wear a wet suit?

A: *Deuteronomy 22:11, "Thou shalt not wear a garment of divers sorts."*

Q: What kind of tree do forefathers grow on?

A: *An ancest-tree.*

Q: Where is the disappearance of the automobile prophesied in the Bible?

A: In Isaiah 3:18–19, which says, "In that day the Lord will take away . . . their round tires . . . , the chains, . . . and the mufflers."

Q: How can you catch righteous diseases?

A: From strait and narrow pathogens.

Q: Which person in the Bible was the son of a fish?

A: Boaz, son of Salmon. (Ruth 4:21.)

Q: Why does the world need Ammon right now?

A: *Because Ammon was good at reducing arms.*

Q: What do you call it when your church responsibility crashes?

A: *A stewardshipwreck.*

Q: How was Boaz blessed when he finally married?

A: He was no longer Ruthless.

Q: What did Laman and Lemuel wear to bed?

A: Lamanightgowns.

Q: Why is the letter *a* like a priesthood meeting prayer?

A: Because it brings men *to* amen.

Q: What do Mormons sing as they make bread?

A: "I Knead Thee Every Hour."

Q: What's black and white and red all over?

A: *Seagulls eating crickets with ketchup.*

Q: Why do people appreciate church spires?

A: *Because spires always have a point.*

Q: What do you get if you have a picnic for thieves and silly insects?

A: Giddy ants and robbers.

Q: How did the Saints keep their ears warm at Winter Quarters?

A: With pion-earmuffs.

Q: What cardiac disease did Laman and Lemuel suffer from?

A: *Heart murmurs.*

Q: What's a good hymn to sing as you go to sleep?

A: *"When upon life's pillows . . . "*

Q: Who fixes the prophet's teeth?

A: The Church Presidentist.

About the Author

Rick Walton has published sixteen joke books and the picture books *Will You Still Love Me?* and *How Many How Many How Many?*

Rick has a B.A. in Spanish/Portuguese, and he has worked as a teacher, an arts administrator, and an educational software designer.

He resides in Provo with his wife, Ann, and their three children.